THE
GREAT
BIG
BOX
BOOK

THE GREAT BIG BOX BOOK

by

Flo Ann Hedley Norvell

photographs by

Richard W. Mitchell

Thomas Y. Crowell   New York

For Papa, Malc, my sisters,
and Edna, the box lady.

Library of Congress Cataloging in Publication Data

Norvell, Flo Ann Hedley. The great big box book.
SUMMARY: Illustrated instructions for a wide variety
of projects using boxes including a log cabin, walkie-
talkie space helmets, and giant building blocks. Also
discusses where to find large boxes and how to transport
them home.
1. Handicraft—Juvenile literature. 2. Boxes—
Juvenile literature. [1. Boxes. 2. Handicraft]
I. Mitchell, Richard, 1949- II. Title.
TT160.N67 1979   745.54   78-22500
ISBN 0-690-03939-5   ISBN 0-690-03940-9 lib. bdg.
FIRST EDITION

Contents

1. Big Box Art

Boxes that are used for sawing ladies in half or for making rabbits disappear are called magic boxes. But aren't all boxes magical? Particularly boxes that are large enough to play in! Sometimes a cardboard box is more fun than the toy it contained.

Here are instructions for turning great big cardboard boxes—the kind refrigerators, ranges, dishwashers, televisions, and other large appliances are packed in—into simple, easy-to-assemble, durable structures that you can use and play in, over and over again. There are directions for making a cannon, a horse, a playhouse, a grocery market, a cash register, giant playing cards, and many more different shapes. The structures are inexpensive—some can be made with a box, a mat knife, a pencil, a yardstick, and some glue—and most of them quickly fold flat for easy storage.

As you learn to make the cylinders, cones, prisms, rectangular columns, and arches that are required for some of the structures in this book, you will start getting exciting project ideas of your own. A rabbit hutch? A doghouse? A robot? A puppet theater? Draw up your ideas, and cut them out in cardboard.

With boxes, you can also move magically backward and forward in time. You can slip backward into an age of knights and castles or of log cabins and tepees, or you can shoot forward into star flights and walkie-talkie space helmets. How would you like to go to the moon? There's a spaceship (chapter 6) that blasts off on balloon power (with a little help from your imagination). Happy landing!

Where to Get Great Big Boxes

Every year in the United States approximately 4.6 million electric refrigerators, 4.1 million automatic washers, 2.8 million dryers, and 3.6 million ranges are sold. All are packed in boxes. After the appliances are unpacked, the boxes are thrown away. This means

1

that over 15 million big boxes are thrown away annually.

Where are these boxes? They are at your nearest catalog store. They are at discount stores in shopping centers. They are at your local appliance and furniture stores. They are at adult retirement communities and apartment complexes or wherever people are moving in and out. In large cities, they are standing on the sidewalks in the warehouse districts and behind department stores in the business districts. In short, they are *everywhere.* You certainly don't need to go out and buy a refrigerator or washer to get a big box!

To get your boxes, call the box source nearest you and ask about refrigerator, range, washer, dryer, and mattress boxes. Or, better still, pay the store a visit. Explain your needs and your project. If you're too shy for this, try the "back door." Go "boxcombing" behind the big discount stores in the shopping centers in the suburbs or behind the big department stores in the cities. You'll be surprised at what you find there. Besides big boxes, you may also find colored poster board, decorative papers, tin buckets, shoe racks, and other useful miscellany. These are the bonuses that come with "boxcombing."

Warning: Don't go "boxcombing" on a trash pick-up day. The boxes will be on their way to the dump. Call your local sanitation department for their pick-up schedule. And don't go on a rainy day either. Wet boxes are useless.

Transporting Your Boxes

You don't need a great big car to get great big boxes to your home or school. A little car will do the job as well. Just take along a pair of pliers and remove the staples that hold the box flaps together. Flatten the boxes and fold them in quarters. Tie them to the roof of your car with light rope and you'll find this method of transporting big boxes is fast and easy.

If you are within walking distance of your box source, simply tie two lengths of rope around your flattened boxes as illustrated. Tie handholds in the ropes and walk your boxes home with the help of a friend.

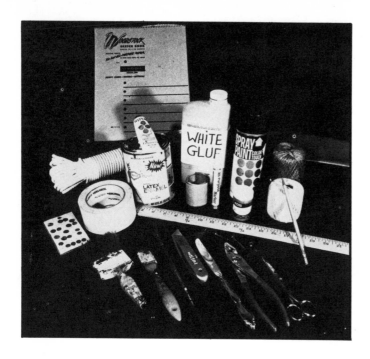

Materials and Tools

A list of materials and tools precedes each project in this book.
Some of the projects require only a mat knife, a pencil, glue a
yardstick, and a table knife. Most households or classrooms
already have many of the other tools and materials you will need,
such as scissors, twine, felt-tip pens, paintbrushes, and wrapping
paper. Here is a list of those materials and tools that you may not
already have on hand.

Boxes: The boxes required for all the projects are made of
corrugated cardboard, which is an especially strong cardboard.
The great big boxes you will need are refrigerator and mattress
boxes and the boxes in which ranges, washers, dryers, and large
television sets are packed. The average refrigerator box measures
67 by 32 by 32 inches. Mattress boxes vary in size but all of them

provide enough cardboard for certain of the larger projects. The average range, washer, dryer, and television box is 28 by 30 by 38 inches. Some projects call for medium-sized and small boxes. The average medium-sized box is about 18 by 17 by 24 inches and the small about 8 by 12 by 12 inches. Don't worry about finding boxes of exactly the right size. You can simply adjust your measurements to suit whatever boxes you have.

Drawing paper: Inexpensive 16-by-20-inch tablets are sold in drugstores, art supply shops, and variety stores. You can often use newspaper or wrapping paper instead.

Glue: Use Elmer's Glue-All, Sobo, or any other fast-bonding white glue. Buy it in a quart size at a hardware or stationer's store. Use a cheap 2-inch paintbrush as a glue brush.

Mat knife (sometimes called a utility knife): Some mat knives come with a retractable blade for safety and portability. Purchase one at a hardware, variety, stationer's, or art supply store. Buy extra blades, which can be stored inside the handle. Always change a dull knife blade immediately.

Paint: You can use one of several kinds of paints. For projects that you plan to leave outdoors, use a gloss or semi-gloss *latex enamel.* Latex enamels come in many colors and can be purchased in quarts and pints. Allow two quarts for the larger projects. The pints are handy for painting the trim. Spray enamels can also be used. Allow three cans of spray enamel for the larger projects. When durability and waterproofing are not essential, it may be cheaper to use *tempera, casein,* or *poster paints.* Purchase these at art supply, variety, or stationer's stores. You can also use tubes of *acrylic paints.* These are water-based pigments packed like oil paints, which come in a variety of colors, and are good for smaller paint jobs like designs and lettering. Purchase them at art supply and stationer's stores.

Paper fasteners: These come in several lengths. Sizes are specified for each project. Purchase them at a stationer's store.

Rope: Use clothesline or sisal rope approximately ¼ inch in diameter. It is sold at hardware or variety stores in 25- and 50-foot lengths.

Tape: When masking tape is called for, use the 2- or 2½-inch-wide variety. Or use brown paper packaging tape. Purchase it at hardware or stationer's stores.

Twine: Use the same kind of twine that you use for wrapping packages for mailing. Purchase it at a hardware, variety, or stationer's store.

Yardstick: A *hardwood* or metal yardstick is more durable than a regular softwood yardstick and can be used for cutting, scoring, and folding, as well as measuring. Purchase it at a stationer's or hardware store.

Tips to Make Big Box Art Easy

Where to Work: A large flat space is all that is required. You can work outside in the yard, park, or school playground, or you can work inside on the garage, classroom, or kitchen floor.

Using a cutting board: In order to protect surfaces when cutting cardboard, always use a cutting board under your work. You can make such a board from another piece of cardboard or from a piece of plywood or Masonite. A good size is 20 by 30 inches.

To cut cardboard: Always use a mat knife. Mat knives are safest because so little of the blade is exposed. For a good clean cut, place a yardstick along the line to be cut. Press down on the yardstick to hold it in place, but keep your fingers and thumb away from the cutting blade. Grip the mat knife in your cutting hand and, holding it at a slant, run it lightly along the yardstick. Increasing your pressure on the mat knife each time, run it along the yardstick two more times.

Scoring cardboard: Scoring is simply making a shallow indentation or cut. If you want to fold a piece of cardboard, you must score it first in order to fold it in a neat, straight line. Place

7

Cutting, scoring, and folding
cardboard.

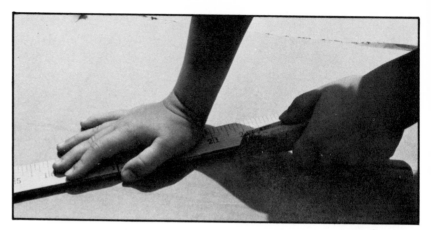

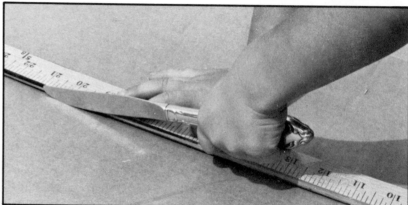

the yardstick along the line to be scored. Run the blade of a dull knife, such as a table knife, back and forth along the edge of the yardstick. Press down firmly on the knife. After scoring, hold the yardstick against the line and fold the cardboard toward you. Fold it away from you. Bend it back and forth several times where greater flexibility is needed.

Punching holes and inserting paper fasteners: To insert paper fasteners, punch holes in the cardboard first by twisting the sharp end of a pair of scissors back and forth. Hold your hand well away from the hole to be punched. Punch holes and insert the paper fasteners one at a time. On most of the bigger projects, instead of paper fasteners, you may use twine if you wish. Just punch two holes instead of one. The holes should be 3 inches apart. Thread twine through the holes and tie in a bow.

Gluing: Apply glue to large areas with a 1- or 2-inch paintbrush and cover the cardboard surface thoroughly. To hold the shapes together while the glue dries, tie them with twine. Drying time for most white glues is approximately 30 minutes.

Marking and adjusting measurements: Use a pencil to mark your measurements and to draw lines on the boxes. On the boxes in the photographs in the book, felt-tip pens and markers were used to make it clear where you are to cut and score. However, heavy black lines such as these will show through a coat of paint. Your measurements will depend upon the size of your boxes or the size of the inhabitant of the boxes. For smaller boxes and smaller children, reduce the measurements proportionately.

Eyeballing: If you're in a hurry and don't care to measure, put away your yardstick and do your measurements with your eye. Study the photographs and then cut the necessary shapes out

9

freehand. You can "eyeball" the playhouse, the castle, the log cabin, the playing cards, the tepee, the horse, the knight's sword and shield, and the hopscotch. Although your "eyeballed" projects may be a bit crooked, they will be nonetheless charming. You should, however, measure projects like the cash register and the giant building blocks, where an exact fit is important.

The printing on boxes: If your box has printing on the outside, and you are not going to paint your project, you may want to turn the box inside out. To do this, cut down one corner of the box, fold it inside out, and reseal the corner edges with 2-inch-wide packaging or masking tape. Or glue a long, 3-inch-wide strip of wrapping paper over the open corner.

Painting your projects: For a quick and easy paint job on the larger projects, use a paint roller and tray. A 2-inch-wide brush

works well for painting the trim. Latex enamels and spray paints will protect your big box structures from light rains and heavy dews, but in case of a torrential downpour, fold up your castle, playhouse, or log cabin and scurry for shelter.

Transfering patterns: Some of the projects require that you make a drawing that is like the one in the book, only much larger. To do this, take a sheet of paper and rule off a series of squares. Look at the diagram in the book. It will tell you how many squares to draw. The text will tell you how large they should be. Draw each line of the pattern across each of your squares in exactly the same position the line is in the diagram. Of course, if you wish, just copy the design in the book freehand, without using the squares. Or you can draw your own pattern.

11

2. Playhouse and Playhouse Furniture

BOXES: For the playhouse, one refrigerator box, one range box, and one small box for the chimney. For the playhouse furniture, five medium-sized boxes (see pages 16 and 17) and one piece of cardboard, approximately 20 by 26 inches.

MATERIALS: Mat knife, pencil, yardstick, table knife, large black felt-tip pen, glue, glue brush.

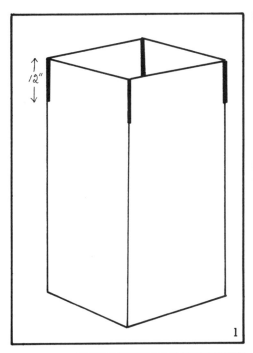

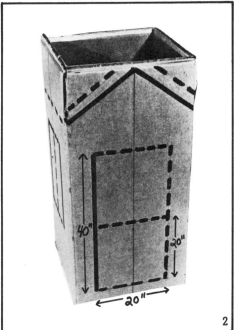

1 To make the playhouse, trim the top and bottom flaps from the refrigerator box. Cut down 12 inches at each corner.

2 With a pencil, draw a line down the center of each of two opposite sides of the box. These sides will be the front and the back of the playhouse. From the bottom of the 12-inch slots, draw the slanted lines for the roof peak on both the front and back of the box. Add 3-inch margins as shown. On the front of the box, using the center line as a guide, measure and draw a 20-by-40-inch rectangle 3 inches above the bottom edge of the box. This will be the door.

3 On each of the two playhouse sides, draw a line down the center. From each center line, measure and draw a 16-by-24-inch rectangle 26 inches above the bottom edge of the box. Divide the rectangle in half lengthwise as shown. Draw the horizontal line 12 inches down from the top.

4 Cut along the dotted lines on

all four sides of the box. Score and then fold along the heavy solid lines. Your box will now look like this.

5 If you want to add window panes and door moldings, draw rectangles in the center of the windows and door as shown. Indent the rectangles 1½ inches for the panes and 2 inches for the door panels. Draw over the pencil lines with a heavy black felt-tip pen.

6 To make the playhouse roof, trim the top and bottom flaps from the range box. Cut the range box in half as shown. Use one half for the roof. Use the other half for the roof shingles. Cut 3 inches off the two bottom edges of the roof piece as shown. Do not trim the shingle piece.

7 On the shingle piece, mark and draw six rows of five shingles each. Cut out the shingles.

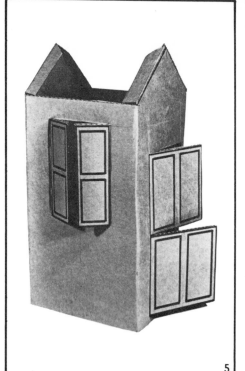

5

6

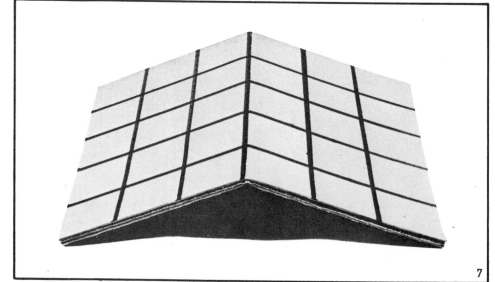

7

14

8 Lay the roof piece flat. Brush glue across the top and bottom of one side of each shingle. Press into place as shown, leaving space between the shingles. Let the second row slightly overlap the first. When all the shingles are in place, walk across them to press them down.

9 To make the chimney, cut inverted V-shapes in two opposite sides of the small box. The V-shapes should match the slant of the roof peak.

10 Place the roof on the house. Place the chimney on the roof and move in. The roof will stay in place without gluing. And if you don't glue the roof in place, you will be able to fold the whole playhouse flat for storage.

15

PLAYHOUSE FURNITURE

1 To make each chair, you will need a small box that fits inside a larger one as shown. These are easy to find. The two boxes used here measure 12 by 10 by 6 inches and 18 by 14 by 9 inches.

2 Trim the flaps from the larger box. Cut out one end of the box. Glue down the flaps at the top of the smaller box. Brush glue on the three sides and the top of the smaller box, turn it upside down, and press it firmly into the larger box. Glue one of the flaps from the larger box onto the top of the smaller box to reinforce the seat. Measure and draw the rectangles as shown. The exact size of the rectangles will depend on the size of your box. Draw the curved lines.

3 Cut out the chair as shown. Sit down!

4 To make the table, trim the loose flaps from the top of the third box and turn the box upside down. The box used here measures 19 by 12 by 12 inches. Measure and draw the

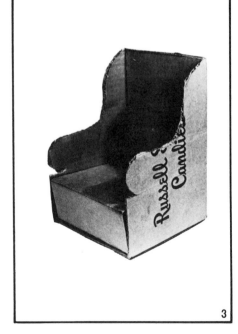

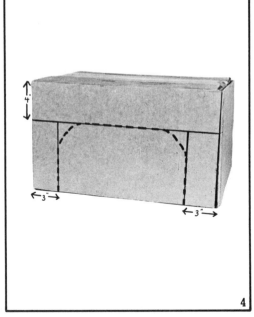

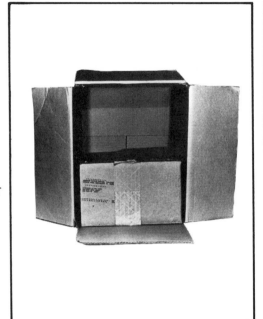

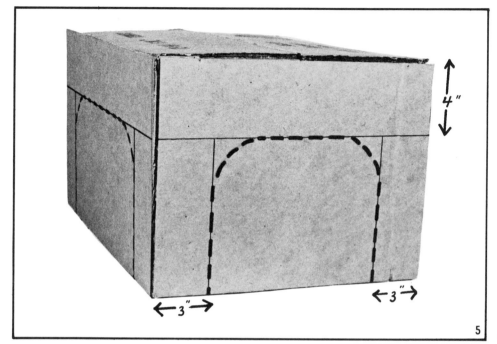

rectangles as shown on the two long sides of the box. Draw the curved lines as shown. The exact measurements will depend on the size of your box.

5 Measure and draw the rectangles as shown on the two ends of the box. Draw the curved lines as shown. Cut on the dotted lines on all four sides of the box.

6 Measure, draw, and cut out a rectangle that is larger on all sides than the table top. Round off its corners and glue the rectangle to the table top. Set the table for supper. When the weather is gloomy and you'd rather play indoors, move your furniture inside the playhouse.

Note: If you want to paint your playhouse, roll on one color and then paint the windows, doors, and flowers (or whatever decorations you choose) in a bright contrasting color. Paint the chimney box red. Outline the bricks with black paint. If you like, you can paint the chairs and table a bright yellow, red, or blue.

3. Indian Tepee and Headdress

BOXES: For the tepee, one refrigerator, mattress, or similar-sized box.

MATERIALS: Pencil, yardstick, mat knife, scissors. For the tepee: thumbtack, string, table knife, 36-inch piece of twine. For the headdress: one piece of approximately 16-by-20-inch drawing paper, black felt-tip pen, 6 drinking straws, glue, cellophane tape, paper clips.

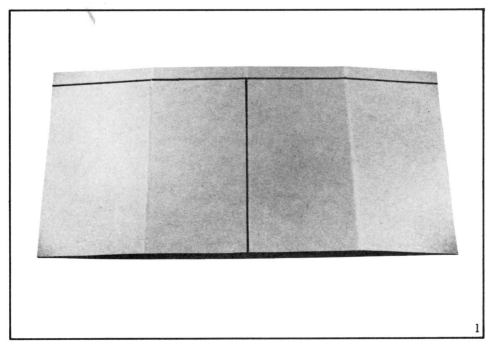

1   To make the tepee, trim the top and bottom flaps from the box. Cut down one corner and spread the box out flat. Draw a line parallel to and 4 inches down from the top of the flattened box. Draw a line lengthwise down the center of the box.

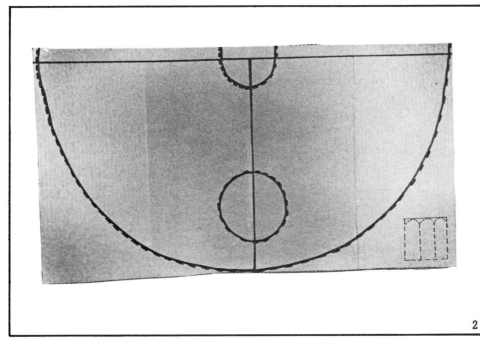

2   Draw a large half-circle for the tepee shape. (Chapter 17 shows how to draw circles.) Make the radius of the circle equal to the length of the center line. At the top of the tepee shape, draw a small half-circle with a 6-inch radius. For the door, draw a circle with a 9-inch radius. Measure and draw three 2-by-12-inch rectangles for the tepee sticks. Cut along the dotted lines, as shown, and round off the corners of the tepee sticks.

3 With your eye, divide the tepee shape into eight parts and draw lines for scoring. Score and then fold along the lines. Bend the cardboard back and forth several times along the lines.

4 Glue the sticks on the inside of the tepee as shown.

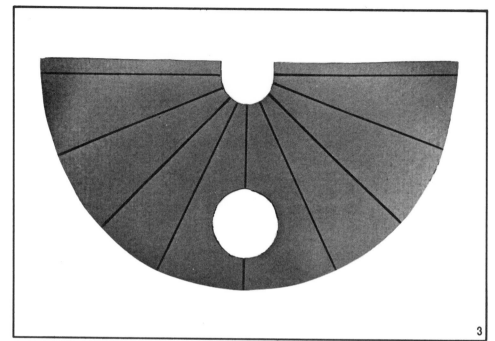

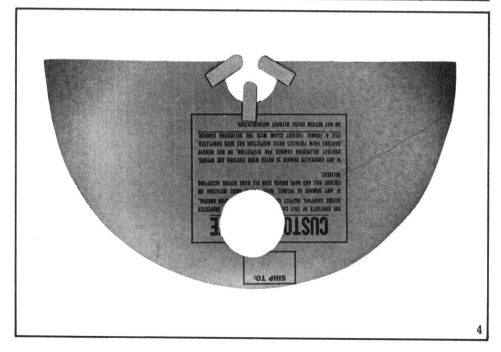

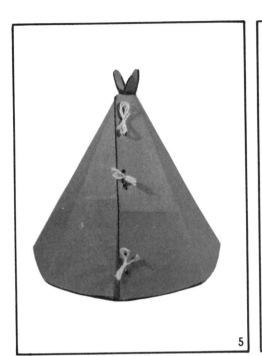

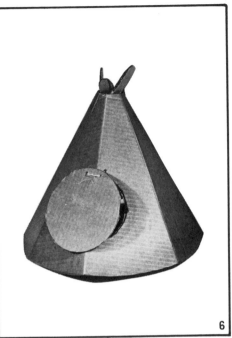

5

6

7

5 Fold the half-circle into a tepee. Punch holes and fasten the overlapping edges with twine.

6 Draw a circle with an 11-inch radius or large enough to cover the doorway of the tepee. There should be enough cardboard left over from the tepee box to do this. Punch two holes at the top of the circle. Punch two holes to match above the tepee door. Thread a piece of twine through the door and tie the ends together in a knot inside the tepee. The twine should be loose enough to allow the door covering to move back and forth.

7 If you wish to paint your tepee and tepee door, do so while they're flat. Roll on a coat of light-colored paint and decorate them with Indian designs in blue, red, or black. To draw the Indian design around the bottom of the tepee, cut two small cardboard triangles as shown. Use them as patterns. Draw around the large triangles and then place the small triangle pattern inside the large triangles and draw around it. Fill in with a solid color. On one side of the tepee, use a ruler to draw a horse. On the other side of the tepee, draw a circle and encircle it with small triangles. Fill in with solid color. To draw the decoration for the tepee door, place your hand in the center of the door and draw around it. Fill it in with a solid color. Sketch the design shown on either side of the hand and fill in with the same color.

INDIAN HEADDRESS

1 Cut a 2-inch-wide strip of drawing paper long enough to go around your head. Allow for a 2-inch overlap. If your head is big, glue two strips together. With a black felt-tip pen, decorate the band with an Indian design. To make the design shown, draw three slanted vertical lines with a ruler. Draw four horizontal triangles on the third line. Repeat the design around the band.

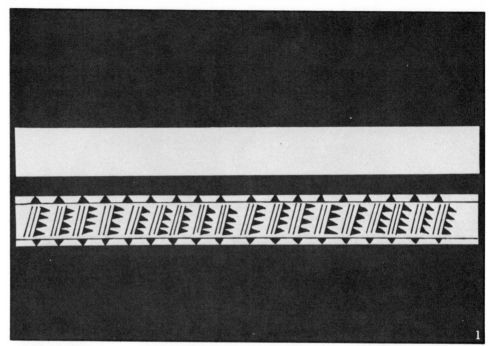

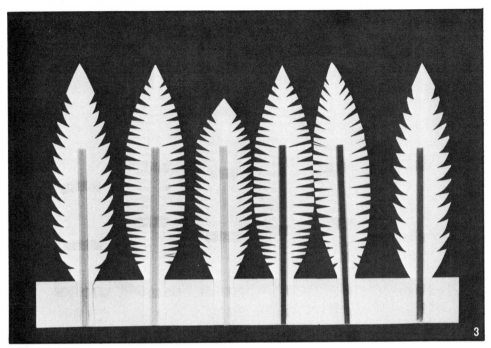

2 Cut six 3-by-12-inch rectangles from the leftover drawing paper. Fold each piece in half lengthwise. Draw a feather pattern on each one as shown. Cut out and cut v-shapes up and down the feathers. Do not cut through the fold. Glue straws on the backs of the feathers.

3 Glue the feathers to the back of the band. For added security, tape the straws to the feathers and to the band.

4 Fold the band of feathers into a circle and glue the ends together. Hold the band together with paper clips until the glue dries.

23

4. Horse

Boxes: Two medium-sized boxes, one slightly larger than the other.

Materials: Mat knife, pencil, yardstick, thumbtack, string, penny, cap from small jar, table knife, glue, glue brush, four 16-by-20-inch sheets of drawing paper (approximately), scissors, cellophane tape, 3 yards of light rope or clothesline, four 1-inch paper fasteners.

1 Trim the bottom flaps from the smaller of the two boxes. The boxes used here measure 18 by 24 by 17 inches and 17 by 12 by 13 inches.

2 Draw and cut a circle in the center of the top of the smaller box. (Chapter 17 shows how to draw circles.) Make the circle big enough to fit around your waist. Use the penny as a pattern and draw and cut a small circle for the tail in one of the box ends.

3 Use the penny again and draw and cut four holes for ropes, one at each corner of the box top. Cut a slot (approximately ⅛ by 6½ inches) for the horse's neck in the other box end.

4 Cut the two larger sides from the second box and on the unprinted surface of one of the box sides, draw two rectangles as shown. Make the horse's neck about 6½ by 13½ inches and the horse's head about 7 by 15½ inches. Round off the corners of the head as shown.

(*Note:* Measurements depend upon the size of the box and can vary proportionately.) Draw two 2½-by-4-inch rectangles for the ears. Round off the corners. Use a cap from a small jar and draw two circles for the eyes. Cut out the horse's neck and head in one piece. Cut out the eyes and the ears.

5 On the *printed* surface of the second box side, draw and cut out another head exactly like the first one. Draw a slanted line as shown on each neck. Score along the slanted lines. Glue the printed sides of the head and neck pieces together. Do not glue section "A." Cut a small hole for the bridle as shown.

6 For the mane, match up two rectangles of the drawing paper. Fold them in half lengthwise. For the tail match up the other two rectangles of drawing paper. Fold them in half crosswise. Cut slits as shown. Curl the slit paper with the scissors blade. (*Note:* If you prefer a hardier mane and tail, you can make them out of rags, using the same cutting method. Old sheets or shirts make good manes and tails.)

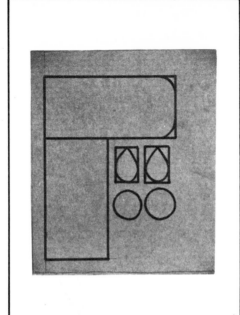

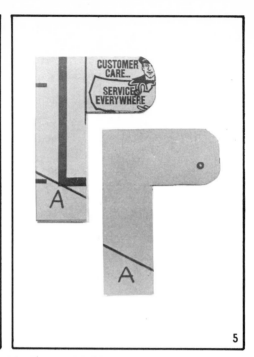

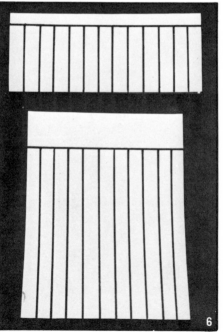

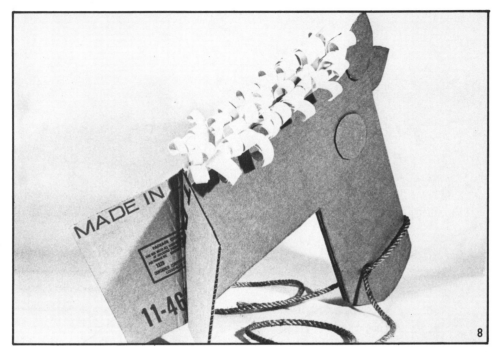

7 Roll the horse's tail into a cylinder shape and tape the overlapping edges.

8 Glue the eyes and ears on either side of the horse's head. String the rope for the bridle through the hole in the horse's nose as shown. Glue the mane to the top of the horse's neck. Fold the scored sections back and forth.

9 Insert the horse's neck into the box slot. Fold back sections "A" in opposite directions inside the box, punch holes, and fasten each section with two paper fasteners. Insert the tail into the hole in the box end and tape in place. Thread ropes of equal length through the holes in the top of the box and knot both ropes at each end. Climb into the box. Pull the ropes over your shoulders. Grab hold of the reins and giddiaaaaaaaap!

Note: To paint a calico pony, brush the body and head with a coat of light-colored paint before you attach ropes. Draw different sized blots with a pencil and fill in the blots with black paint.

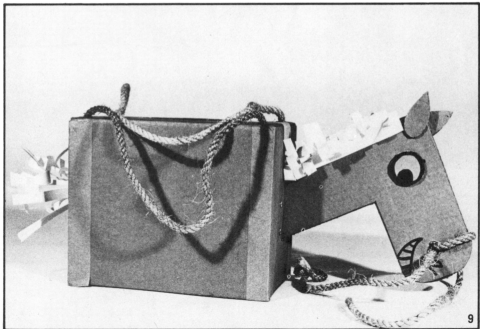

5. Cannon

BOXES: One range, washer, dryer, or similar-sized box, one cardboard carpet roll, and one medium-sized box approximately 12 by 17 by 10 inches. (*Note:* if you can't find a cardboard cylinder around which carpets are rolled, substitute a range or similar-sized box, approximately 30 by 38 inches.)

MATERIALS: Mat knife, pencil, yardstick, thumbtack, string, glue, glue brush, table knife, two broomsticks, saw, one large topless vegetable or fruit can (#2½), hammer, nail.

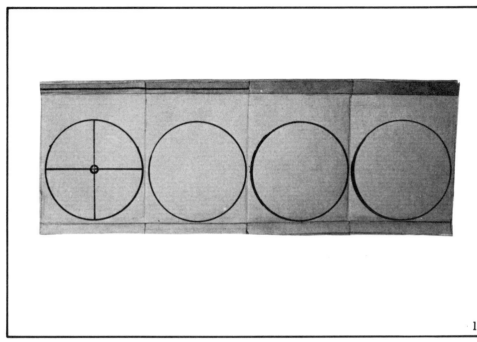

1 To make the two cannon wheels, cut off the flaps, cut the range box down one corner, and spread the box out flat. On one of the four sides of the box, draw and cut out one large circle (Chapter 17 shows how) with a radius of approximately 12 inches. Cut a hole the size of the broomstick in the middle of the circle. Use the large circle with the hole in the middle as a pattern and cut out three more. Glue the circles together in twos.

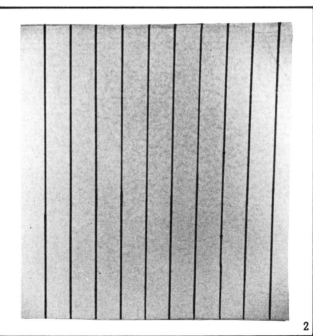

2 To make the cannon barrel from the carpet roll, simply cut the roll to a 36-inch length. To make the barrel from the range box, trim the flaps from the top and bottom of the box. Cut down one corner and flatten the box. Cut a rectangle approximately 25 by 36 inches. With a pencil, divide the rectangle into equal vertical sections as shown. Score and then fold along the solid lines. Bend the cardboard back and forth several times along the lines.

3 Roll the scored piece into a cylinder and glue the overlapping edges. Tie with string to hold in place until the glue dries.

4 To make the cannon body, take the medium-sized box and cut circles in the box ends lettered "A" so that the cylinder will fit snugly. Cut a hole the size of your broomsticks at the bottom of each side lettered "B."

5 Insert the cylinder in the holes as shown. Cut four 2-by-24-inch rectangles from scrap cardboard for bands. Wrap a band around either end of the cannon barrel as shown and glue the overlapping edges. Tie with string to hold in place until the glue dries. Save two bands for the wheels.

3

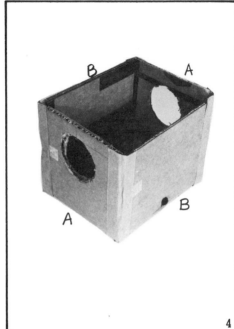

4

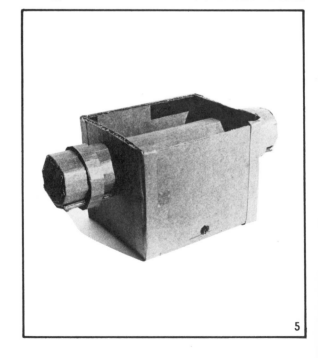

5

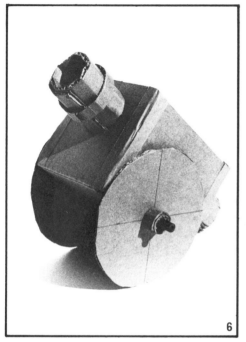

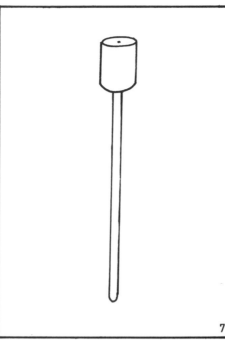

6 Cut one of the broomsticks for an axle and insert it in the cannon box. Put the wheels on the broomstick. (*Note:* if you are going to paint your cannon different colors, paint the wheels before putting them on the axle.) Brush one side of each of the two bands with glue and wrap the bands around the axle to hold the wheels on. Tie with strings to hold them in place until the glue dries.

7 To make the plunger, brush the top of the second broomstick with glue and nail the large can to it. Make sure the can is slightly smaller than the inside of the barrel.

8 Used tennis balls make harmless cannon balls. Load one at a time. Insert the plunger into the cannon and fire away.

6. Flying Saucer Spaceship

BOXES: One refrigerator, mattress, or similar-sized box.

MATERIALS: Mat knife, pencil, yardstick, thumbtack, string, table knife, penny, scissors, thirty-one 1½-inch paper fasteners, two empty cardboard tubes from rolls of wax paper or wrapping paper (the longer the better), giant balloons.

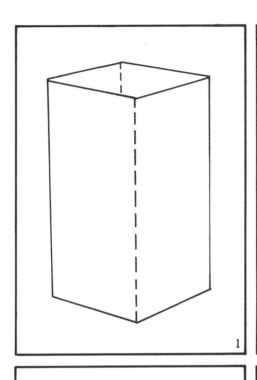

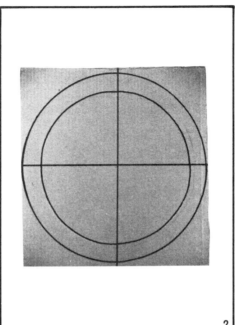

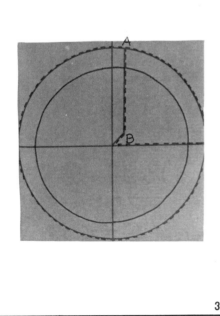

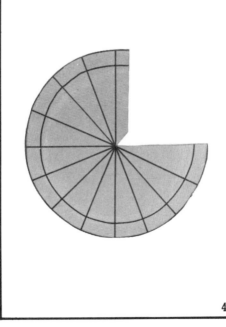

1 Trim the top and bottom flaps from the box. Cut along the dotted lines and spread the box out flat.

2 On the unprinted surface of one box half, draw lines down the center, crosswise and lengthwise. Then draw a large circle with a radius equal to one-half the width of the box half. Inside the larger circle, draw a circle that is 5 inches smaller in radius. (Chapter 17 shows how to draw circles.)

3 The spaceship is made from two shallow cones. (Chapter 17 shows how to make cones.) Measure and mark a 4-inch flap at points "A" and "B." Cut along all the dotted lines.

4 Divide the circle into twelve equal parts (approximately) and score and then fold along these lines. You can divide with the eye if you wish. Bend the cardboard back and forth several times along the scored lines.

5 Divide the rim of the circle as shown. Cut away the shaded sections, lettered "B." This is the top of the spaceship.

6 Use the piece that you have cut as a pattern to draw the bottom half of the spaceship. Place the pattern on the *printed* side of the other box half. Draw around it. Mark the center. Mark and score the bottom piece exactly as you did the top. Sketch in the "B" tabs and cut away the sections lettered "A."

7 On the spaceship top, use a mat knife to taper the tabs lettered "A." Draw a circle with an 8-inch radius for the door. Cut on the dotted line. Do not cut out the top of the circle. Score a line at the top of the circle and fold out the door. Cut out two smaller circles the same size as your cardboard tubes.

8 On the spaceship bottom, trim the "B" tabs to taper them. Draw the two half-circles for the windows, using a 6-inch radius. Cut on the dotted lines. Score along the lines marked "X." Draw and cut out the three

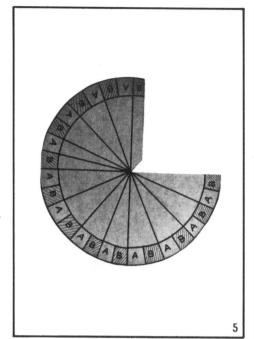

5

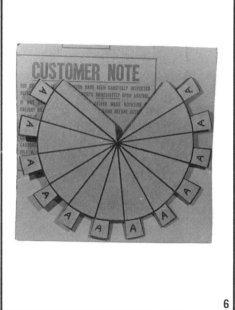

6

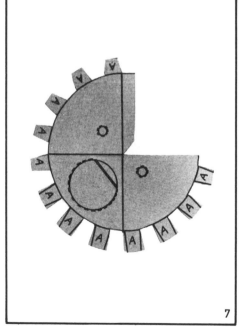

7

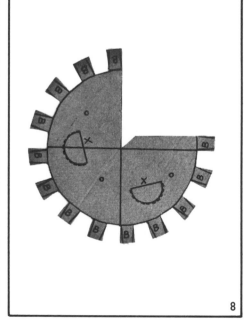

8

smaller holes. Each should be the size of a penny.

9 The two halves of the spaceship now look like this. Fold these two halves into cone shapes and fasten each with paper fasteners along the overlapping flaps.

10 Match up the overlaps and fit the cones together so that the sections interlock. Fasten the tabs with paper fasteners. After half of the sections are fastened, one person can get halfway inside the spaceship to help in bending back the last of the fasteners. Insert the cardboard tubes for the telescopes. Blow up the balloons and wrap rubber bands around the necks. Insert the balloons in the penny-sized holes. Giant balloons mean more power. When your spaceship is ready for lift-off, remove the rubber bands and let the air out of the balloons. Your imagination will take you the rest of the way.

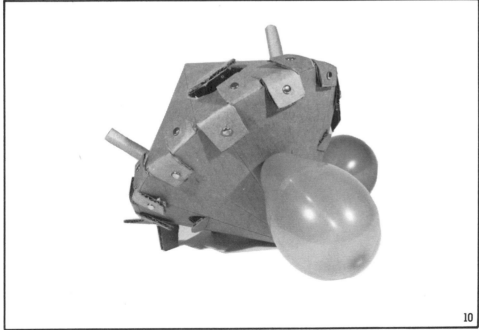

Note: To paint your spaceship, choose two contrasting colors and paint every other scored section a different color.

7. Walkie-Talkie Space Helmets

BOXES: Two boxes large enough to fit over your head and roomy enough to be comfortable.

MATERIALS: Pencil, six topless soup or tunafish cans, top from a catsup bottle, mat knife, glue, glue brush, hammer, nail, 40 feet of string, 2-inch-wide masking tape.

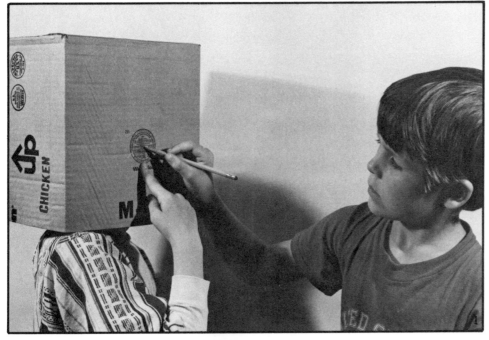

1 Trim the flaps from the tops of the boxes and put a box over a friend's head. Have your friend point to his or her ears, mouth, and eyes. Mark these spots with a pencil.

2 Center the tin cans over the ear and mouth marks and draw around the cans with a pencil. Place the bottle top over each eye mark and draw around it.

3 Cut out the ear, mouth, and eye holes. Cut smaller circles in the discarded ear circles. These doughnut shapes will go over the eye holes.

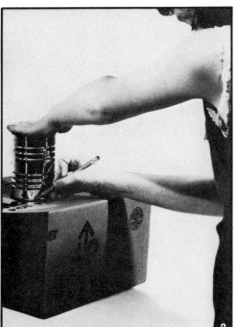

37

4 With a hammer and nail, punch a hole in the center of four of the cans.

5 Thread a 20-inch piece of string through the ear and mouth cans as shown. Tie the string ends around a wooden match, a twig, or a rolled piece of paper.

6 Cut a piece of masking tape to fit around a can. Cut slits in the tape. Then place the masking tape around the can as shown.

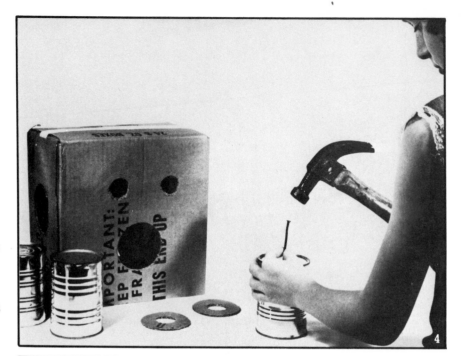

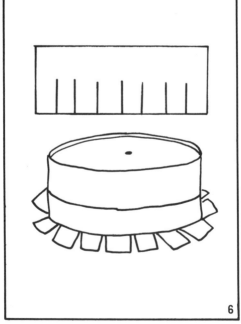

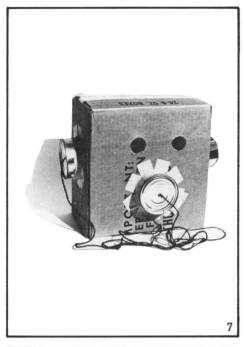

7

7 Push the cans into the box holes so that about a half-inch of each can is inside the box. Press the slit tape against the boxes as shown. Glue the doughnut shapes you made over the eye holes.

8 Wire the communication strings as shown. Now you are ready to communicate with your spaceship. When you speak over the walkie-talkie, be sure the string is stretched taut.

Note: You can paint your helmets if you like, but only after you have taped the cans to the boxes. Masking tape does not hold well on a painted surface.

8

8. Pup Tent

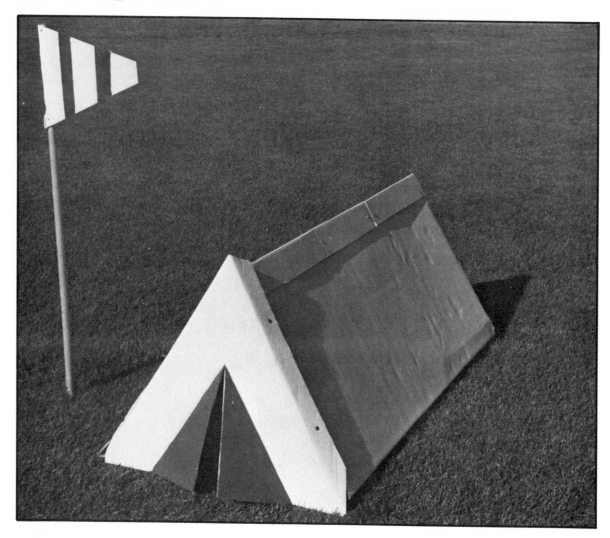

BOXES: One refrigerator or other large box and one medium-sized box.

MATERIALS: Mat knife, pencil, yardstick, table knife, glue and glue brush (or twenty-two 1½-inch paper fasteners and scissors for punching holes), 6 yards of string, broomstick, carpet tacks, hammer.

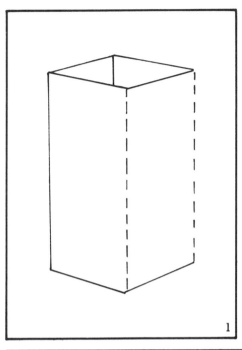

1 Trim the top and bottom flaps from the large box and cut away one side of the box. Save the cut-away side.

2 Trim the edges of the box sides lettered "A" so that they are equal in length and width.

SICO INCORPORATED

7525 CAHILL RD.
MINNEAPOLIS, MINN. 55435 U.S.A.

A   A

'ABLE DANCE FLOOR

2 PANELS #21510 OAK
2 PANELS #21610 TEAK

3 Trim the flaps from the top of the smaller carton, as shown in figure A. Cut down each corner along the dotted lines. Flatten the box as shown in figure B. Cut two long 8-inch-wide rectangles along the dotted lines for the tent roof flaps. Score down the center of each rectangle as shown in figure C. Fold by bending the cardboard back and forth along the scored line. (The tent roof flaps can be made from any discarded cardboard but should be at least 8 inches wide.)

4 Brush the roof flaps with glue. Fold the large, three-sided box section into a triangle and place the flaps over the open side as shown. Tie strings around the tent to hold the flaps in place while the glue dries. If you want to be able to pack the tent flat for storage, use paper fasteners instead of glue to hold the flaps in place.

5 Turn the tent on its end and place it on the cut-away side of the big box, as shown. Draw two triangles the same size as the two tent openings.

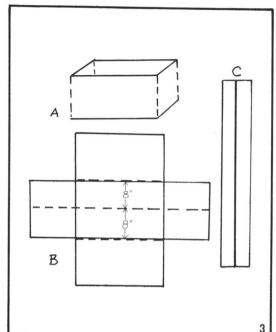

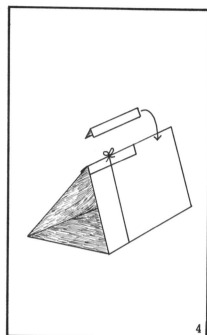

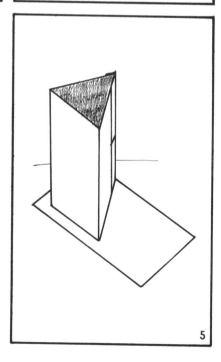

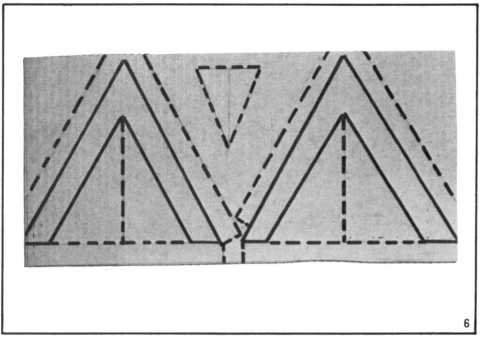

6 Add 3-inch margins around the three sides of the triangles. Draw smaller triangles for the doors. (Chapter 17 shows how.) Each triangle should be about 16 inches high with a 20-inch base. Draw a triangle for the flag 12 inches high with a 10-inch base. Cut along the dotted lines. Score and then fold along the solid lines. Bend the cardboard back and forth several times along the scored lines.

7 Glue (or fasten with 1½-inch paper fasteners) the door pieces to the front and back of the tent as shown.

8 Write your name on the flag or decorate it with a design and glue or tack it to the broomstick. Find a good place for your campsite and pitch your tent and stake your flag.

Note: To make your tent weather resistant, paint it with two coats of high-gloss latex enamel. Paint both sides of the floor. If your tent is too hot in the summer, leave one end open and glue mosquito netting across it.

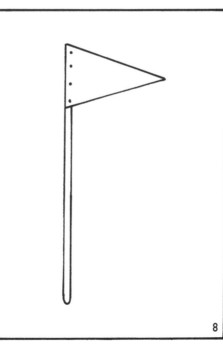

9. Castle

BOXES: Two refrigerator boxes and one range box.

MATERIALS: Mat knife, pencil, yardstick, 6-by-24-inch piece of drawing paper (or wrapping paper or newspaper), scissors, quarter (25¢), table knife, sixteen 1½-inch paper fasteners, thumbtack, string, glue, glue brush, four 8-foot lengths of rope or clothesline.

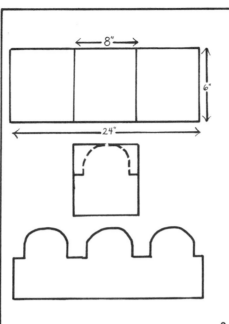

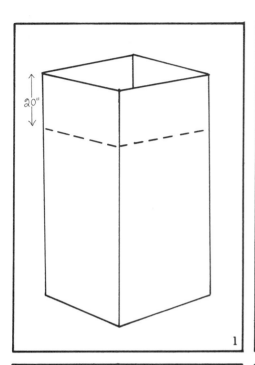

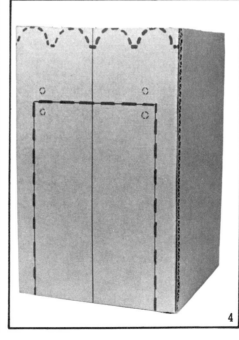

1 To make the drawbridge section of the castle, cut the flaps from the top of one of the refrigerator boxes. Do not cut off the bottom flaps. Measure and draw a line as shown on all four sides of the box. Cut along the dotted line. Reserve the cut-away piece for pennants.

2 To make a pattern for the scallops at the top, fold the 6-by-24-inch piece of paper into thirds. On the folded paper draw the shape as shown in the diagram. Cut along the dotted line. Unfold the pattern.

3 Hold or tape the pattern against the box as shown. Draw around the scallops. Use the pattern to draw scallops all the way around the box.

4 For the drawbridges, on each of two opposite sides of the box, draw a vertical center line. From this center line measure and draw a 24-by-36-inch rectangle. Using a quarter, draw small circles at the top corners of each drawbridge, and matching circles above, in the castle wall.

5 On each of the two other sides of the box, draw a vertical center line. From the center line, draw a 12-by-36-inch rectangle 4 inches above the bottom edge of the box. Draw the curved lines. Cut along all the dotted lines as shown.

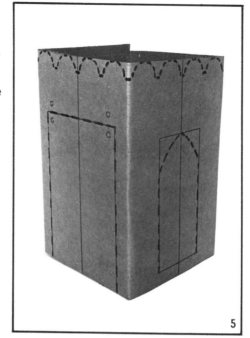

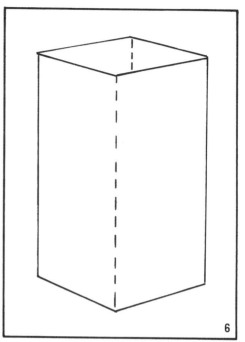

6 To make the bottom sections of the two towers, cut off the top and bottom flaps of the second refrigerator box. Cut the box in half along the dotted lines, as shown. Lay the two pieces out flat.

7 With a pencil and yardstick, divide each piece into equal vertical sections (approximately 6 inches wide) and draw lines as shown. Score and then fold along the lines. Bend the cardboard back and forth several times along the lines.

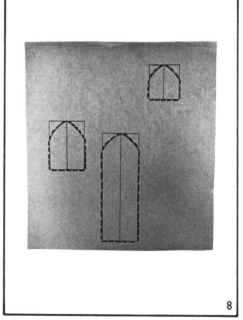

8 Measure and draw the door rectangle (12 by 36 inches) in the center of each piece, 3 inches above the bottom edge as shown. Draw the large window rectangle (12 by 16 inches) and the smaller window rectangle (10 by 12 inches) as

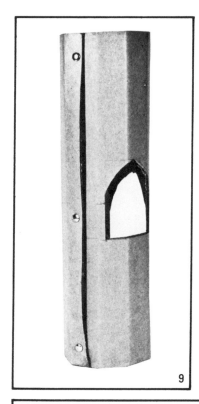

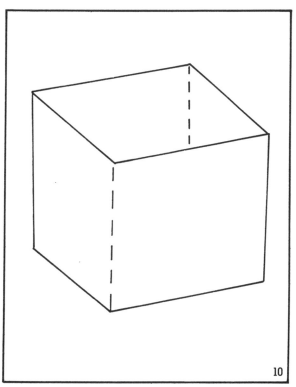

shown. Draw the curved lines. Cut along all the dotted lines.

9 Roll the two scored pieces into cylinder shapes. Overlap the edges 6 inches and punch three holes in the top, middle, and bottom of the overlap. Secure with the paper fasteners.

10 To make the two cone-shaped tower roofs, cut the range box in half along the dotted lines.

11 On each half draw a semicircle and flap. (Chapter 17 shows how to make a steep cone.) The radius of the semicircle should be approximately 29 inches. Cut along the dotted lines and score and then fold along the solid lines.

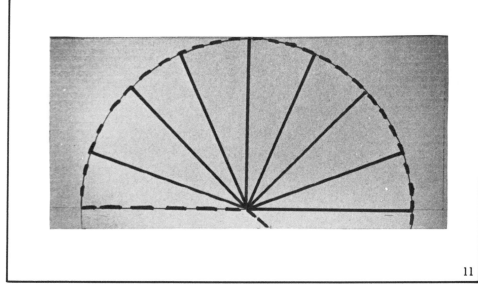

9

10

11

12 Roll the two pieces into cone shapes. Punch holes in the overlapping flap and secure with paper fasteners. Cut a 3-inch slot in the top of the front of each one to hold the pennants.

13 To make the pennants, cut four 20-by-24-inch cardboard rectangles from the piece left over from the drawbridge box. Measure and draw four pennants as shown. Each square equals 4 inches. Cut the pennants out and glue them together in twos for added strength.

14 To assemble the castle, punch holes in the sides of the drawbridge box and the two towers. Attach each of the towers to the drawbridge box with three paper fasteners. Put the cone roofs on the towers. (If you want to attach the roofs to the towers, punch holes in each

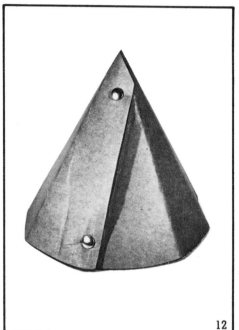

12

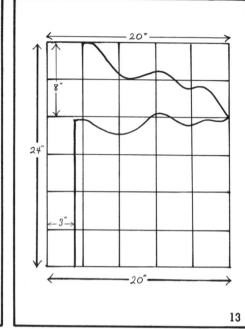

13

14

side of the two cones and in the tower bottoms and thread with twine. Tie knots.) Insert the pennants in the roof slots. Thread the lengths of rope through the holes in the drawbridge section. Knot the ropes at both ends. Find a moat and put your castle at the edge of it. Lower and raise your drawbridge as guests arrive and leave.

10. Knight's Shield, Sword, and Helmet

BOXES: For the two shields, two medium-sized boxes measuring at least 20 by 24 by 20 inches. For the two swords, one medium-sized box at least 24 inches high and 20 inches wide. For the two helmets, one medium-sized box measuring at least 20 by 18 by 8 inches.

MATERIALS: Mat knife, pencil, yardstick, scissors. For the shields, glue, glue brush, 2 feet of heavy twine. For the swords, one 10-by-24-inch piece of drawing paper (or wrapping paper or newspaper), glue, glue brush. For the helmets, one 18-by-20-inch piece of drawing paper (or wrapping paper or newspaper), table knife, one 4½-by-15-inch piece of drawing paper (or wrapping paper or newspaper), four 8½-by-11-inch sheets of drawing or typing paper, cellophane tape or masking tape, eight 1-inch paper fasteners.

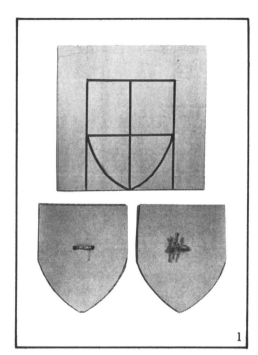

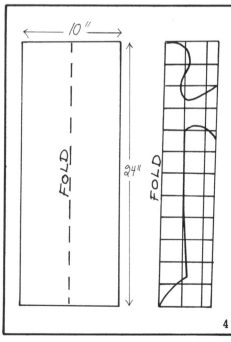

1 To make the two shields, cut four 20-by-24-inch cardboard rectangles. On one of the rectangles, measure and draw the lines as shown. Cut out the shield shape. Use this piece as a pattern and cut three more shield shapes. Glue the shields together in twos. Punch holes for the handle and thread with sturdy twine as shown. Tie the ends of the twine together. Leave enough space to get your hand through the twine.

2 If you wish, paint your shields with a solid color and then add a design in a contrasting color. The stripes in this design are 3 inches wide.

3 If you like, you can make a knight's cross design. Paint the shield with a solid color and then measure and draw the cross as shown, or draw it freehand. Paint the cross in a contrasting color.

4 To make the two swords, first cut four 10-by-24-inch pieces of cardboard. Then fold the 10-by-24-inch piece of paper in half. Transfer the sword pattern as shown, or draw your own sword. Each square equals 2 inches. (Chapter 1 tells how to transfer a pattern.) Cut out the pattern and unfold it. Trace around the pattern on one of the pieces of cardboard.

5 Cut out the sword. Using this sword as a pattern, cut out three more. Glue the swords together in twos. For added strength, glue a 1-inch-by-⅛-inch stick along the back of the sword.

6 To make the two helmets, first cut two 18-by-20-inch pieces of cardboard from your box. Then, on the 18-by-20-inch piece of drawing paper, measure and draw the shape as shown.

7 Cut along the dotted lines of the pattern. Then use the pattern to cut two helmet shapes from the 18-by-20-inch pieces of cardboard. Score and then fold along the heavy solid lines indicated on the pattern.

8 On the 4½-by-15-inch piece of paper, measure and draw the shape shown for the visor. Cut along the dotted lines. Using the pattern, cut two visor shapes from two pieces of cardboard.

5

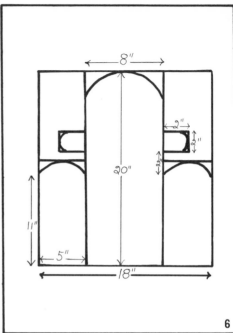

6

7

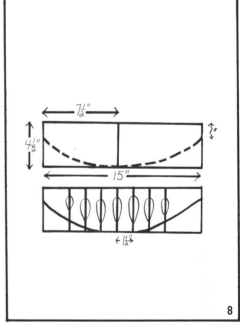

8

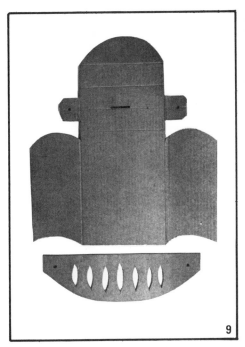

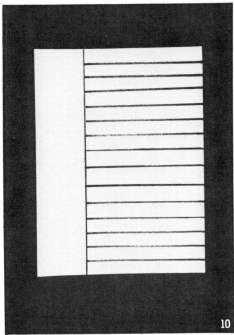

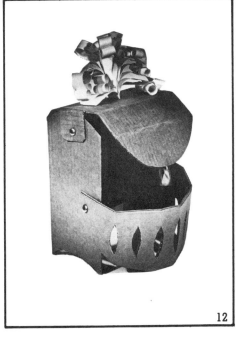

9 Punch holes in the helmet tabs. Punch holes in each end of the visor. Cut a slot for the plume.

10 To make the plume for the helmet, fold two of the 8½-by-11-inch sheets of paper together. With a pair of scissors, cut into strips as shown. Cut two plumes.

11 Roll the double-sheeted plumes into two cylinder shapes. Wrap the uncut section with tape. On each side, cut a slot halfway up the taped section. Curl the cut strips with the edge of the scissors.

12 Fold the helmet together and attach the tabs to the helmet with paper fasteners. Attach the visor as shown. Place pieces of cellophane tape or masking tape over the shanks of the fasteners inside the helmet. Insert the plume in the top of the helmet. Fold back the stem on either side and tape to the top of the inside of the helmet. You are now ready with your helmet, shield, and sword to guard the castle's drawbridge properly!

11. Grocery Market and Cash Register

BOXES: For the market, one refrigerator box and one small box from which to make the fruit bin. For the cash register, one washer, dryer, or range box. Two of the box sides should measure at least 38 by 30 inches.

MATERIALS: Mat knife, pencil, yardstick, table knife, scissors. For the market, four 1½-inch paper fasteners. For the cash register, one 30-by-38-inch piece of wrapping paper, cellophane tape, nickel or bottle cap, six 1-inch paper fasteners, glue, glue brush, 12-inch piece of twine, four spring-type clothespins or a large rubber band, penny, small sheet of white paper, black felt-tip pen.

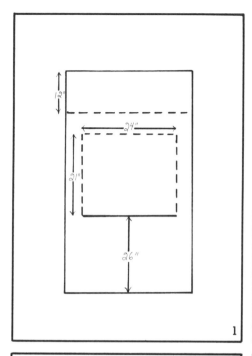

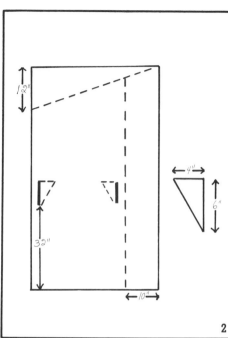

1 Trim the top and bottom flaps from the refrigerator box. Save the flaps for shelves. On the front side of the box, measure and draw the lines as shown.

2 On the two box sides, measure and draw the lines as shown.

3 Cut along all the dotted lines. Score along the solid lines.

4 On the piece you cut away from the back of the box, measure and draw the awning as shown.

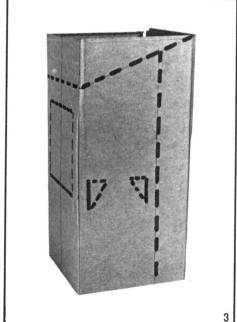

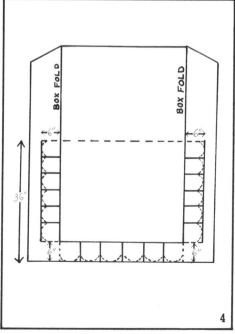

5 Cut along the dotted lines. Score along the solid lines.

6 Measure and draw the lines on the counter as shown. Score along the heavy solid lines. Bend the cardboard back and forth along the lines and fold the counter toward the inside of the box, in the directions indicated by the arrows.

7 Fasten the bottom of the counter to the market with paper fasteners as shown. Put the flaps on the triangle supports for shelves.

8 To make the fruit bin, measure and cut the small box as shown.

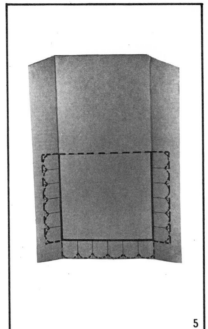

5

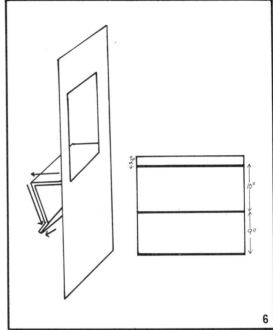

6

7

8

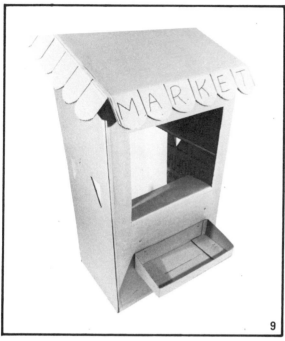

9

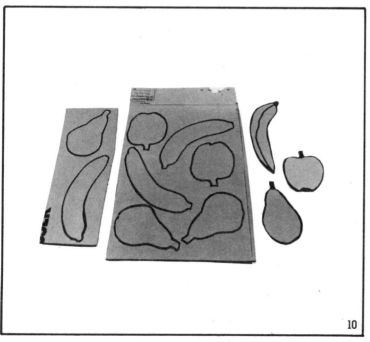

10

9 Punch holes in the back of the fruit bin and attach to the market with paper fasteners as shown. Place the awning on top of the market. If you like, you can attach it to the market at each corner with paper fasteners or heavy twine. Stock your market with empty gelatin and cereal boxes, empty soup and vegetable cans, and empty milk cartons. You can glue the tops back together on the boxes and cartons.

10 To stock your fruit bin, use a black felt-tip marker to draw pear, banana, and apple shapes on a piece of cardboard. Cut the fruit out with a mat knife and decorate it with the marker. Now that your market is stocked, you're ready for customers!

Note: The market is easily disassembled and can be stored flat. To paint the market, roll on a coat of white or light-colored paint. Paint the stripes on the edges of the awning and the fruit bin in a contrasting color: blue, red, orange, yellow, green, or black. The awning stripes are 5½ inches wide, those on the fruit bin 3 inches wide.

CASH REGISTER

1 To make a pattern for the cash register, fold the sheet of wrapping paper in half. Draw a 38-by-5-inch rectangle as shown. Measure and draw the horizontal lines. The horizontal lines are all 2 inches apart except where indicated. Draw a curve to join points A, B, and C.

2 Connect the horizontal lines with the vertical lines as shown. With a pair of scissors, cut along the dotted lines.

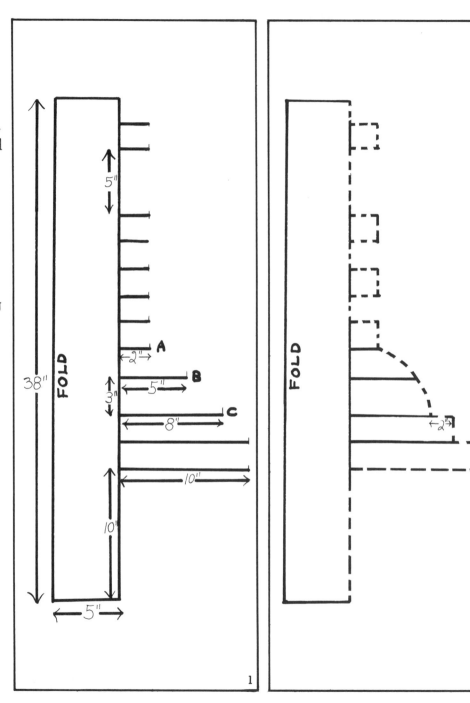

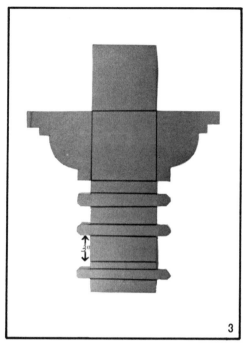

3 Unfold the pattern and tape it to a 30-by-38-inch cardboard rectangle. Draw around the pattern and cut out the cash register shape as shown. Score on the dark solid lines. Bend back and forth on the scored lines.

4 Now draw around a nickel or bottle cap to make three rows of keys. Draw four keys in each row. Make the rows approximately 1½ inches apart. Cut the circles almost all the way around, but do not cut the tops of the circles. Fold the keys out.

5 Punch holes in the six tabs. Fold the cash register together and place it on its back. Punch holes in the sides of the cash register to match the holes in the tabs. Insert paper fasteners in the holes and reach inside to fold back the shanks.

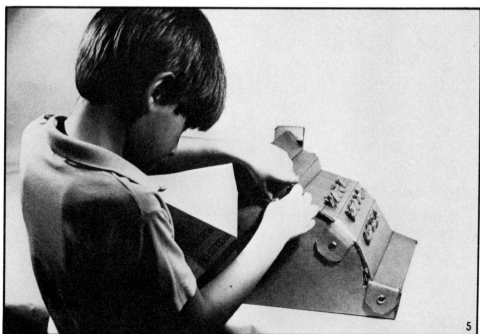

6 Cut two 9½-by-2½-inch cardboard rectangles from cardboard scraps. Score lengthwise down the center of each rectangle. Bend the scored lines back and forth. Glue these strips to the bottom and sides of the cash register as shown.

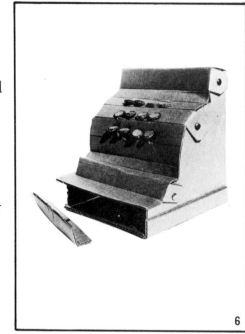

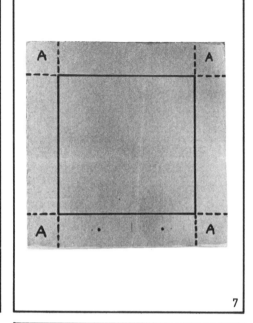

7 To make the drawer, draw a 1½-inch margin around the four sides of a 12½-inch cardboard square as shown. Cut along the dotted lines. Score along the solid lines. Bend back and forth on the scored lines. Punch two holes as shown.

8 Glue the corners of the drawer together. Tuck flaps "A" inside. Hold flaps in place with clothespins or a large rubber band until the glue dries. Thread twine through the holes. Tie knots at both ends.

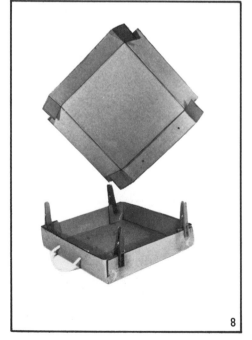

9

10

9 Use a penny to draw twelve circles on a piece of white paper. Draw two 2-by-4-inch rectangles. Letter the Sale signs and number the keys with a black felt-tip pen. Cut out the circles and glue to the cash register keys. Cut out the Sale signs and glue to the front and the back of the cash register.

10 Insert the drawer in the cash register and fill it with play money. Make your own on pieces of paper with a black felt-tip pen or buy some at a variety store. Use a dinner bell or bicycle bell to ring up the sales in your market.

12. Log Cabin

BOXES: One refrigerator box, one range box, and one small box for the chimney.

MATERIALS: Mat knife, pencil, yardstick, table knife, glue, glue brush, large black felt-tip marker.

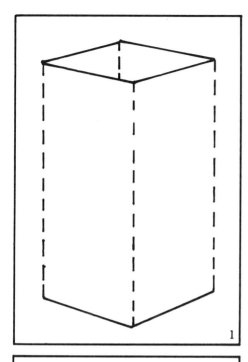

1

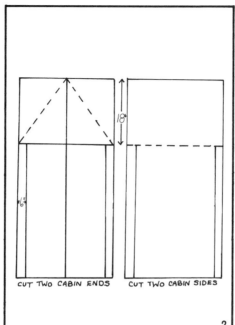

2

CUT TWO CABIN ENDS   CUT TWO CABIN SIDES

18"

6"

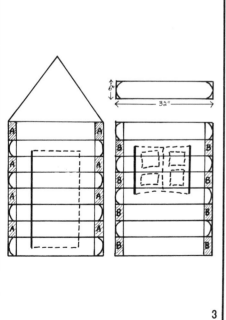

3

32"
6"

A A
A A
A A
A A
A A

B B
B B
B B
B B
B B

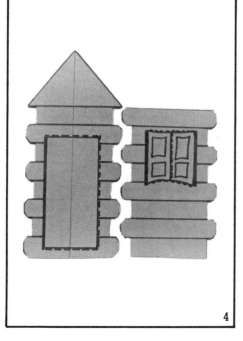

4

1 Trim the top and bottom flaps from the refrigerator box. Cut down each corner as shown by the dotted lines.

2 With a pencil and yardstick, measure and draw the lines as shown on the four box sides. Make two cabin ends with roof peaks and two cabin sides. The parallel lines down each box side are indented 6 inches.

3 From some scrap cardboard, draw and cut a 6-by-32-inch rectangle for a log pattern. Round off the corners. With a pencil, mark off eight logs on each box side. Your log size will vary with the size of your box. On one of the cabin ends, 3 inches from the bottom edge of the box side, measure and draw an 18-by-36-inch rectangle for the door. On the two cabin sides, draw rustic windows freehand. Cut out the shaded sections lettered "A" on the two end pieces. Cut out the shaded sections lettered "B" on the two cabin sides.

4 Cut the door and windows along the dotted lines. Score and fold along the heavy solid lines.

5 Trim the top and bottom flaps from the range box. Cut the range box in half, as shown. Cut off a 3-inch strip from each side of one of the halves. Reserve this half for a roof.

6 Divide the other half into six rows of five shingles each. Cut out the shingles.

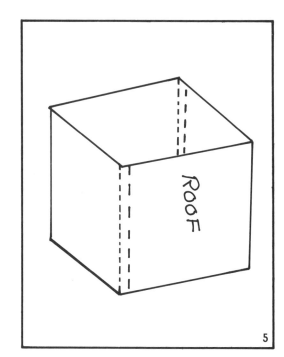

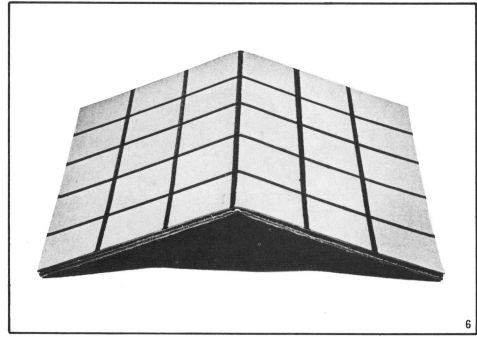

7 Brush glue across the top and bottom of one side of each shingle and lay the shingles on the roof one row at a time. Let each row overlap slightly. Leave space between the shingles. Walk across the shingles to press them down. Let them dry approximately 30 minutes.

8 Use the small box to make the chimney. On two opposite sides of the box, cut an inverted "V" to match the slant of the roof peak.

9 Join the walls of your cabin together by interlocking the logs as shown. Put the roof and chimney on and move in.

Note: If you are not going to paint your cabin beige and dark brown like the one in the introductory photograph, just use your black marker to line the logs, outline the window panes, and sketch out bricks on the chimney. You may also want to add a few knotholes to the logs.

65

13. Giant Building Blocks

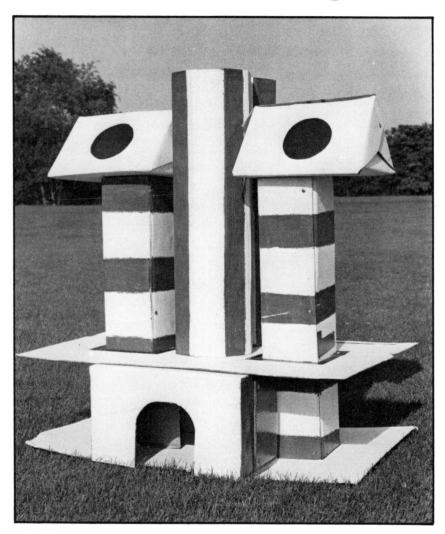

BOXES: One refrigerator or similar-sized box and one range or other large box.

MATERIALS: Mat knife, yardstick, pencil, table knife, glue, glue brush, 6 yards of string.

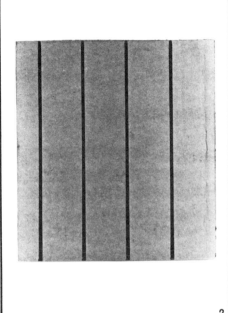

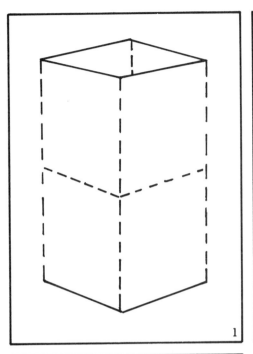

1 Trim the top and the bottom flaps from the refrigerator box. Cut down each box corner as shown by the dotted lines. Cut each box side in half. Trim six of the pieces to measure approximately 32 by 36 inches. Square off the remaining two pieces so that they measure approximately 32 by 32 inches.

2 To make the rectangular column block, use a pencil and yardstick to measure and draw a line 2 inches in from and parallel to the edge of one of the 32-by-36-inch cardboard pieces. Divide the remaining space lengthwise into four equal sections. Score along the dark lines. Fold by bending the cardboard back and forth on the scored lines. Make two.

3 Fold each piece into the shape shown and glue the overlapping edge in place. Tie a string around each block to hold it together while the glue dries. It is not necessary, but if you wish to seal the open ends of the blocks, use pieces of scrap cardboard and cut and fold them as shown.

4 To make the circular column block, use a pencil and yardstick to divide one of the 32-by-36-inch pieces into equal sections lengthwise, as shown. Score along the dark lines. Fold by bending back and forth on the scored lines. Make two.

5 Roll the two pieces into cylinder shapes and overlap and glue the edges of each cylinder. Tie a string around each block to hold it in shape until the glue dries.

6 To make the prism-shaped block, use a pencil and yardstick to draw a vertical and then a horizontal line across the center of one of the 32-by-36-inch pieces. From the two center lines, measure and draw lines as shown.

7 Add the margins lettered "A." Cut along the dotted lines. Make two.

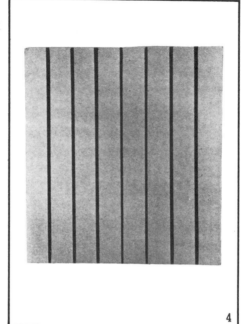

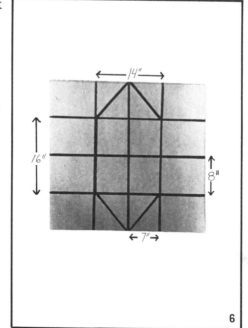

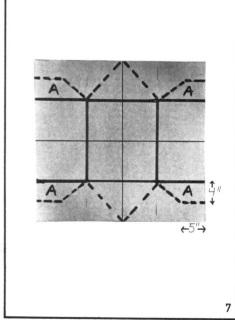

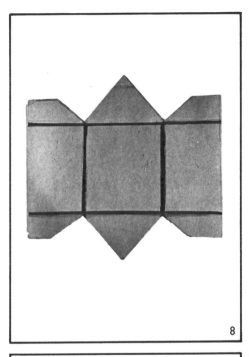

8

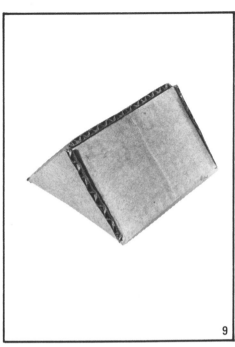

9

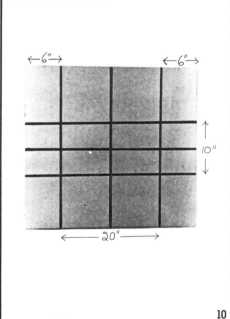

10

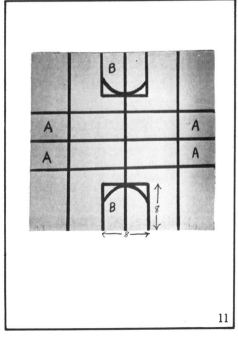

11

8 Score along the dark lines. Fold along the scored lines by bending back and forth.

9 Fold each piece into the prism shape shown and glue the ends. Use plenty of glue, brushing it across the entire surface of each end. Tie a string around each block to hold it together until the glue dries.

10 To make the arch-shaped block, use a pencil and yardstick to draw a vertical and then a horizontal line across the center of one of the square pieces of cardboard. From the two center lines, draw the measurements as shown.

11 Draw the arches as shown. Cut out the sections lettered "A." Cut out the arches lettered "B." Make two.

12 Score along the dark lines.

13 Fold each piece into the arch shape as shown and glue the overlapping ends together. Brush glue across the entire surface of each end flap. Tie a string around each block to hold it together while the glue dries.

14 To make the four cardboard cutouts into which the circular and rectangular columns can fit, trim the top and bottom flaps from the range box. Cut down each box corner as shown by the dotted lines.

15 With a pencil, divide one of the cardboard pieces in half lengthwise and crosswise. Stand the circular-column blocks in the center of each half. Draw around them. Cut out the circular shapes so that the blocks fit snugly into the holes. Make another cutout exactly like this one.

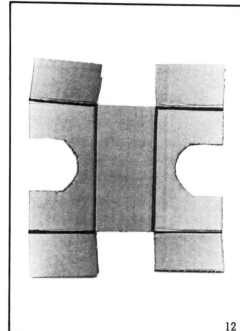

12

13

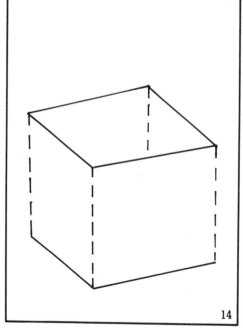

14

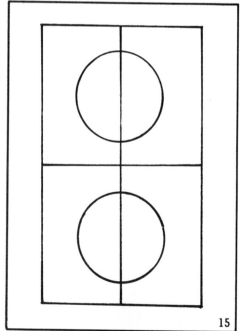

15

70

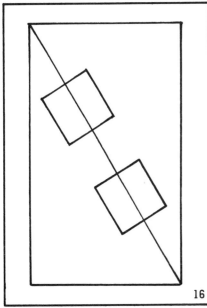

16

16 On another piece of cardboard, draw a diagonal line as shown. Stand the rectangular columns on the diagonal line on the cardboard pieces and draw around them. Cut out the shapes so that the blocks fit snugly into the holes. Make another cutout exactly like this one.

Note: Get some more boxes and make as many blocks as you can. The more the merrier. Paint them, if you like, by blocking off geometric designs with masking tape. Use latex enamels in contrasting bright colors.

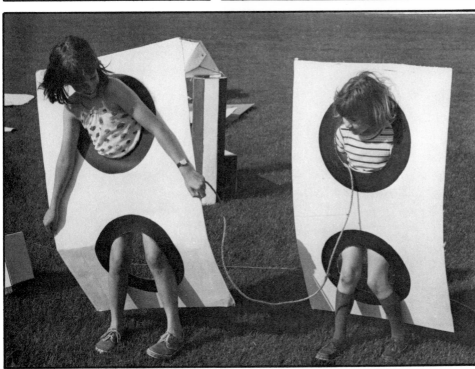

14. Giant Playing Cards

BOXES: One refrigerator or similar-sized box.

MATERIALS: Mat knife, pencil, yardstick, six sheets of drawing paper or typewriter paper, scissors, large black felt-tip marker.

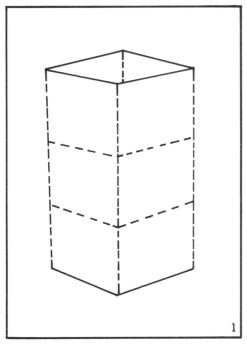

1 Trim the top and bottom flaps from the box. Cut down each corner and divide each box side into thirds. Cut along the dotted lines. From these twelve pieces you will make the cards. They should measure roughly 24 by 32 inches.

2 To make the first card, cut 6-inch slots in the center of the top and the bottom of the card. Make the slots ⅛ inch wide. Then, on each side of the card and equidistant from the center of the card, cut two slots 6 inches long as shown. Round off the corners of the card. Use this card as a pattern and cut eleven more.

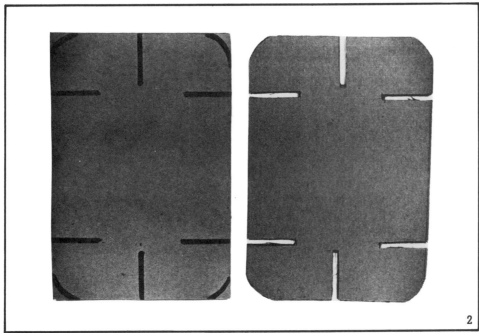

73

3 Cut four 6-by-6-inch paper squares. Cut four 2-by-2-inch paper squares. Fold the larger squares in half and divide them into 1-inch squares as shown. Divide the smaller pieces into ½-inch squares. Transfer the large and small diamond, heart, spade, and club designs to the paper squares. (Chapter 1 tells how to transfer a pattern.) Cut out the shapes and use them as patterns.

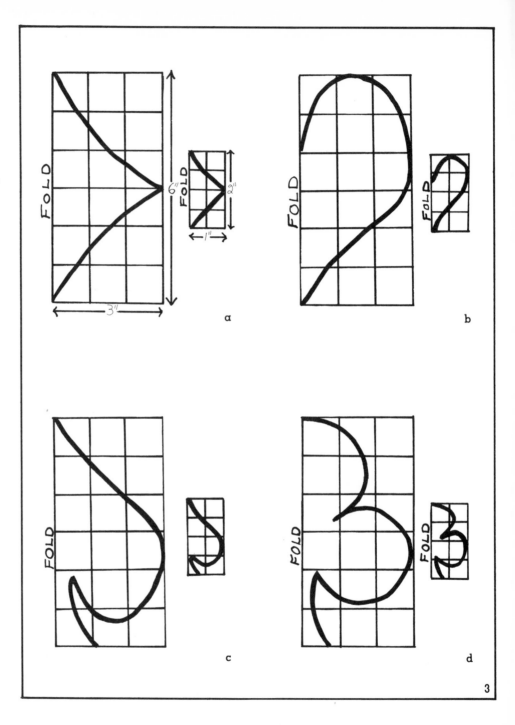

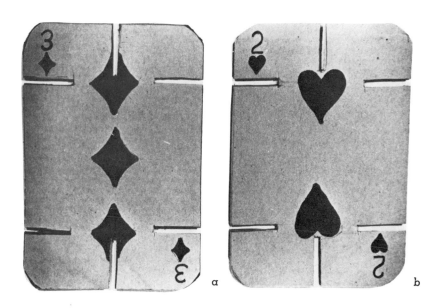

a

b

c

d

4

4 Draw the large and small diamonds, hearts, spades, and clubs on the cards and space them as shown. Fill in the designs with a large black felt-tip marker and add the numbers. Or you can cut the card suits from different-colored pieces of construction paper and glue them on. If you want a larger variety of cards, consult a deck of playing cards for the different designs.

Note: If you wish to paint your cards, apply a coat of white latex enamel paint and let them dry. Then paint the numbers and the suits on the cards with red and black waterproof acrylic paints.

15. Artist's Easel

BOXES: One refrigerator box.

MATERIALS: Mat knife, pencil, yardstick, table knife, glue, glue brush, sixteen 1½-inch paper fasteners.

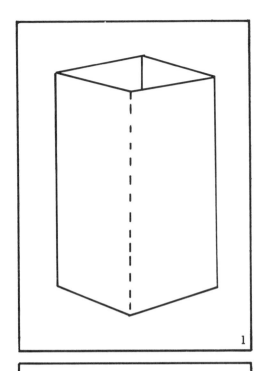

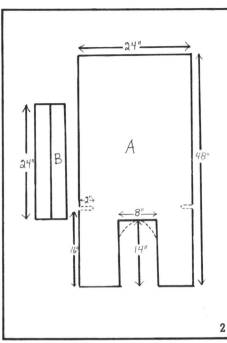

1 Trim the top and bottom flaps from the refrigerator box. Cut along the dotted line and spread the box out flat.

2 Measure and draw one easel shape (A) and one easel hinge (B) on the flattened piece of cardboard. Score the easel hinge down the center and fold by bending the cardboard back and forth on the scored line.

3 Cut out the easel shape. Use this as a pattern and cut one more easel shape.

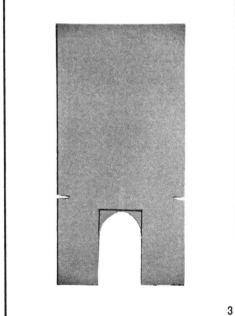

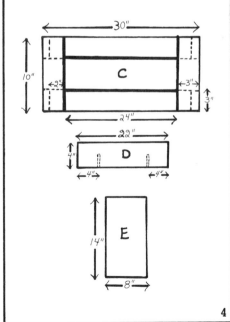

4 Measure and draw the paint tray (C), the brace (D), and the leg piece (E). Cut out the shapes. On the paint tray, cut along the dotted lines to make the tabbed ends. Use each shape as a pattern and cut one more paint tray, one more brace, and three more leg pieces. Cut out the slots in the braces. Score and fold the paint trays along the heavy solid lines.

5 The basic shapes will now look like this.

6 Glue the "E" shapes on the four easel legs. If your box is printed on one side, glue the shapes on the printed side.

7 Punch holes in the hinge (B) and attach it with paper fasteners to the tops of the two easel shapes, as shown.

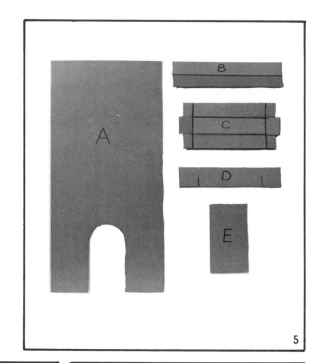

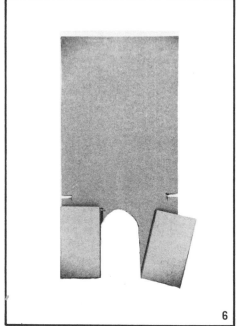

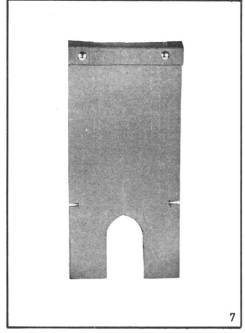

8

8 Fold up the paint trays (C) on the scored lines and fasten the ends together with paper fasteners as shown. Tuck the short flaps inside.

9 Attach the paint trays to each side of the easel with paper fasteners. Insert the braces in the slots in the legs of the easel as shown. Use clothespins to clip pieces of paper to the easel, and start painting! The easel is remarkably durable and can be easily disassembled and stored flat. You can put it together again and again, whenever you feel a "masterpiece" coming on. A coat of latex enamel will make it last even longer.

9

16. Portable Hopscotch

BOXES: Range, washer, dryer, or other similar-sized box.

MATERIALS: Mat knife, pencil, yardstick, table knife, large black felt-tip marker.

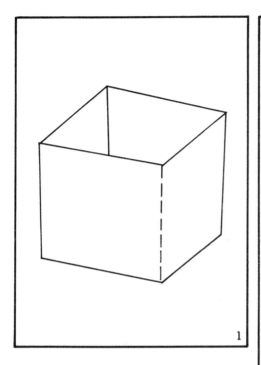

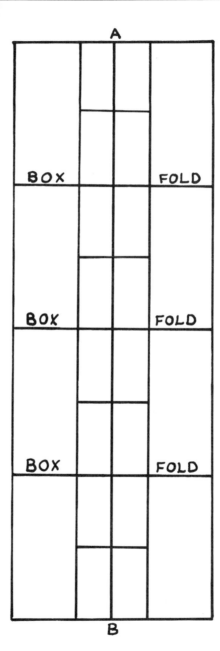

1 Trim the top and bottom flaps from the box. Cut down one corner of the box as shown by the dotted line. Spread the box out flat.

2 With a pencil and yardstick, measure and draw a line (AB) lengthwise down the center of the flattened box. Then draw two parallel lines, each 7 inches from the center line. Divide the center strip into eight squares as shown.

3 Add 6-inch-wide rectangles (lettered "A") on either side of the third, fifth, and seventh squares.

4 Cut along the dotted lines. If you wish to play the regular shorter version of hopscotch, cut off the top two squares.

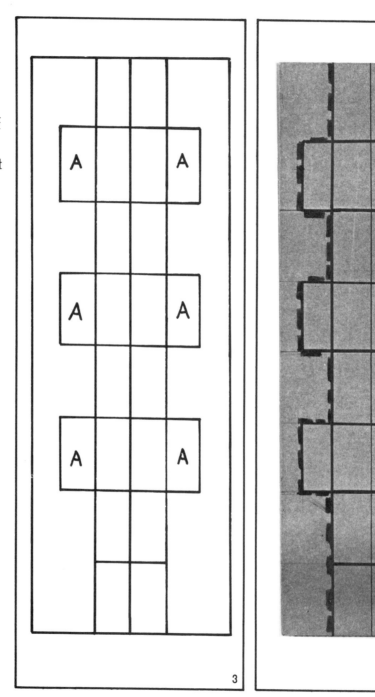

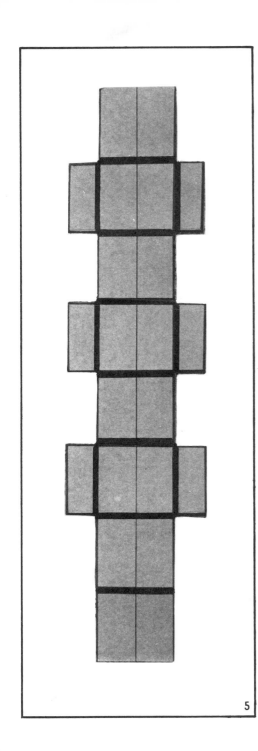

5

6

5 Score along the heavy solid lines.

6 With a large black felt-tip marker and a yardstick, draw lines to divide the squares as shown. Number the hopscotch.

Note: If you wish, paint your hopscotch with a light-colored enamel and add numbers in a darker color.

83

17. Drawing Geometric Shapes

Directions are given here for making squares, rectangles, circles, cones, triangles, and cylinders so that you can use these basic shapes to create your own projects. The projects you can make from great big boxes are as varied as your imagination.

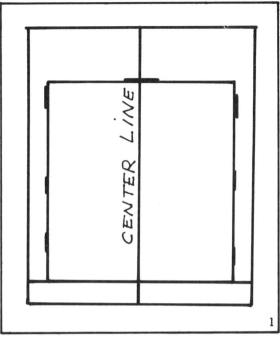

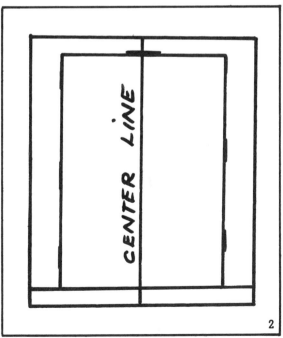

DRAWING SQUARES AND RECTANGLES

1 The simplest way to draw these shapes on boxes is to draw a line lengthwise down the center of the box and then to measure out from the line. For the square, draw a straight line across the bottom of the box side. Draw a line lengthwise down the center of the cardboard. From the center line, mark off at several points on either side one-half the measurement of the square's side. From the bottom of the center line measure up and make a mark equal to the square's side. Connect the marks with straight lines.

2 For the rectangle, draw a straight line across the bottom of the box side. Draw a line lengthwise down the center of the cardboard, and mark off on either side measurements equal to one-half the width of the rectangle. From the bottom of the center line, measure up and make a mark equal to the length of the rectangle. Connect the marks with straight lines.

DRAWING A CIRCLE

1 Divide the piece of cardboard in half lengthwise and crosswise. Measure and mark your radius from point C as shown. (The diameter of a circle is a line passing straight across the center of it. The radius is equal to one-half the diameter.)

2 Place a thumbtack with a string knotted around it on point C. Measure along the string the length of the radius you want. Tie a pencil to the string at this point. Draw the circle by swinging the pencil completely around point C.

DRAWING A SHALLOW CONE

1 The shallow cone is made from three-quarters of a circle. First draw a center line lengthwise and then crosswise on a piece of cardboard. Then draw a circle with the radius you want, as above. Draw a line parallel to and 3 inches from line CX as shown. Mark Y 4 inches from the center line. Draw CY.

2 Cut along the dotted line.

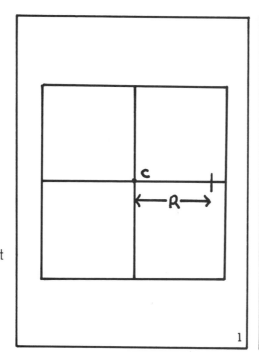

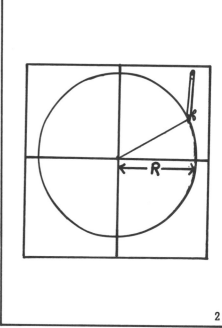

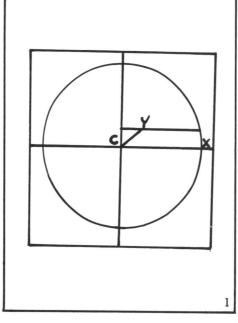

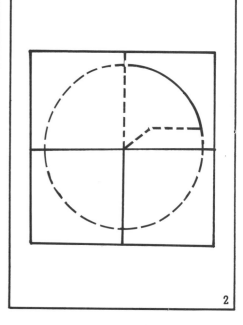

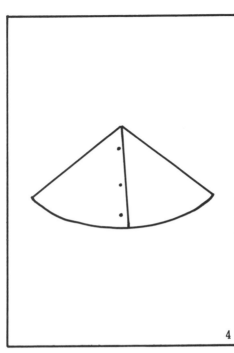

3

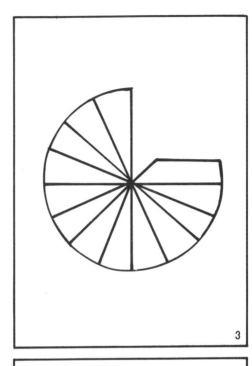

4

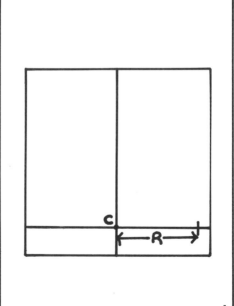

1

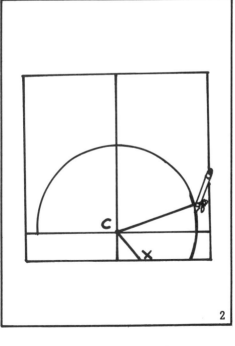

2

3 Divide the shape as shown and score along the heavy solid lines. Fold by bending the cardboard back and forth along the scored lines.

4 Roll into a cone shape and glue together where the edges overlap. Or punch and secure with paper fasteners or twine.

DRAWING A STEEP CONE

1 The steep cone is made from a half-circle. First draw a line down the center of the cardboard. Draw another line parallel to and 3 inches up from the bottom edge of the cardboard. From point C, measure and mark the radius you want, as shown.

2 Place a thumbtack with a string knotted around it at point C. Measure along the string the length of the radius. Tie a pencil to the string at this point. Draw a half-circle by swinging the pencil halfway around point C. Mark X 4 inches from the center line and then draw the line CX.

3 Cut along the dotted line.

4 Divide the half-circle as shown. Score along the heavy solid lines. Fold by bending back and forth on the scored lines.

5 Roll the half-circle into a cone shape and glue the overlapping edges together. Or punch holes and secure with paper fasteners or twine.

DRAWING A TRIANGLE

1 A triangle is a shape with three straight sides. The sides may all be equal or each side may vary in length. An isosceles triangle has two sides that are equal in length. In the drawing, B represents the base of the triangle, H the height.

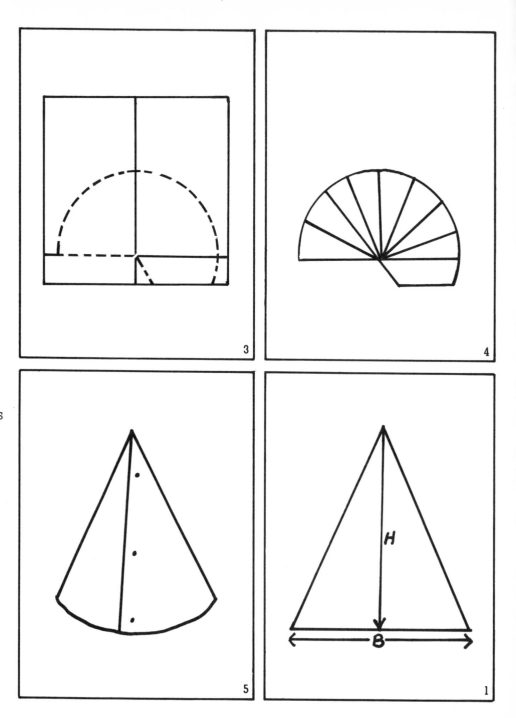

88

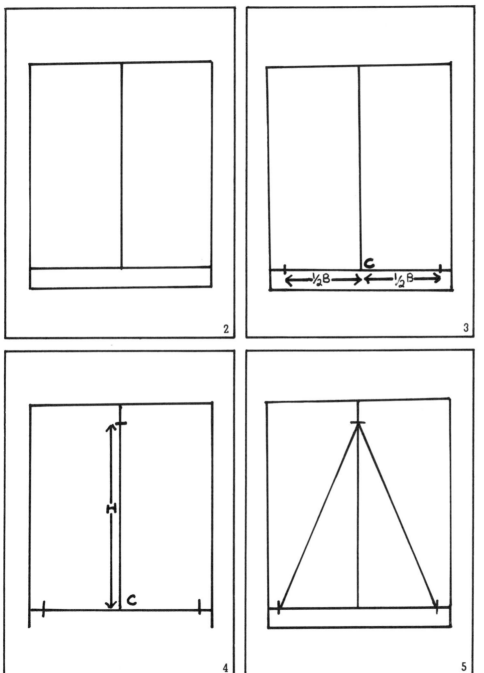

2 To draw a triangle, divide the cardboard in half lengthwise. Draw a base line parallel to the bottom edge of the cardboard.

3 Measure ½ B on either side of point C.

4 Measure the height of the triangle along the center line and make a mark.

5 Join the marks with straight lines as shown.

DRAWING A CYLINDER

1 In big box art, a cylinder is a rectangle of cardboard rolled into a circular shape. The circumference of a cylinder is the distance around it.

2 To make a cylinder, measure and draw a rectangle whose height (H) is equal to the height of the desired cylinder, and whose length is equal to the circumference (C) of the cylinder plus 3 inches.

3 Draw a line parallel to and 3 inches from the side of the rectangle as shown (AB). Divide the rest of the rectangle into equal sections averaging about 6 inches wide. Draw lines and score. Fold by bending back and forth on the scored lines.

4 Roll the rectangle into cylinder shape. Glue the overlapping edges or punch holes as shown and fasten with paper fasteners or twine.

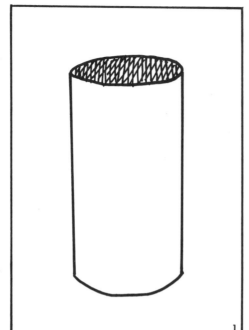

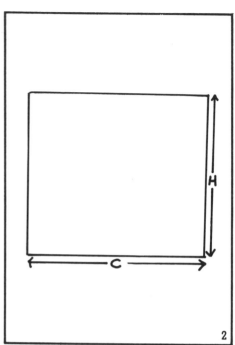

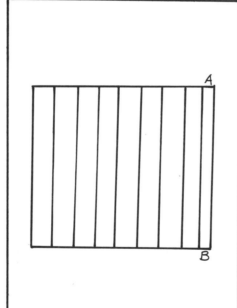

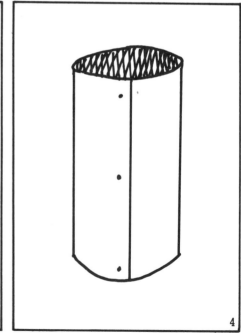